The Giant Turnip

by Joanna Lake
illustrated by Ana Sebastian

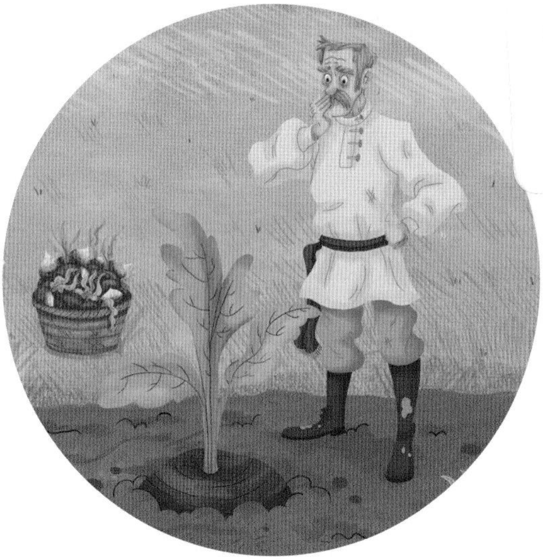

OXFORD
UNIVERSITY PRESS
AUSTRALIA & NEW ZEALAND

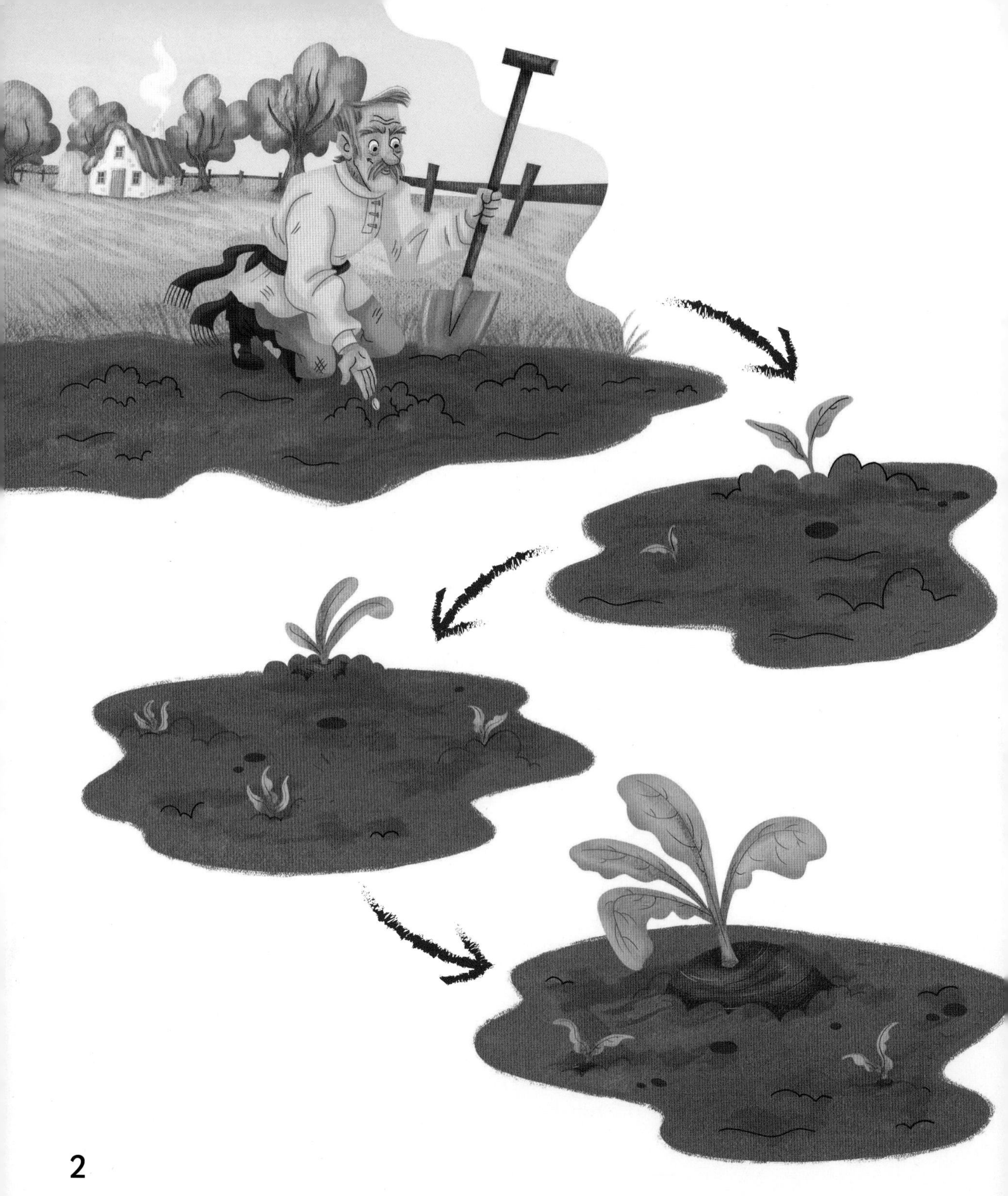

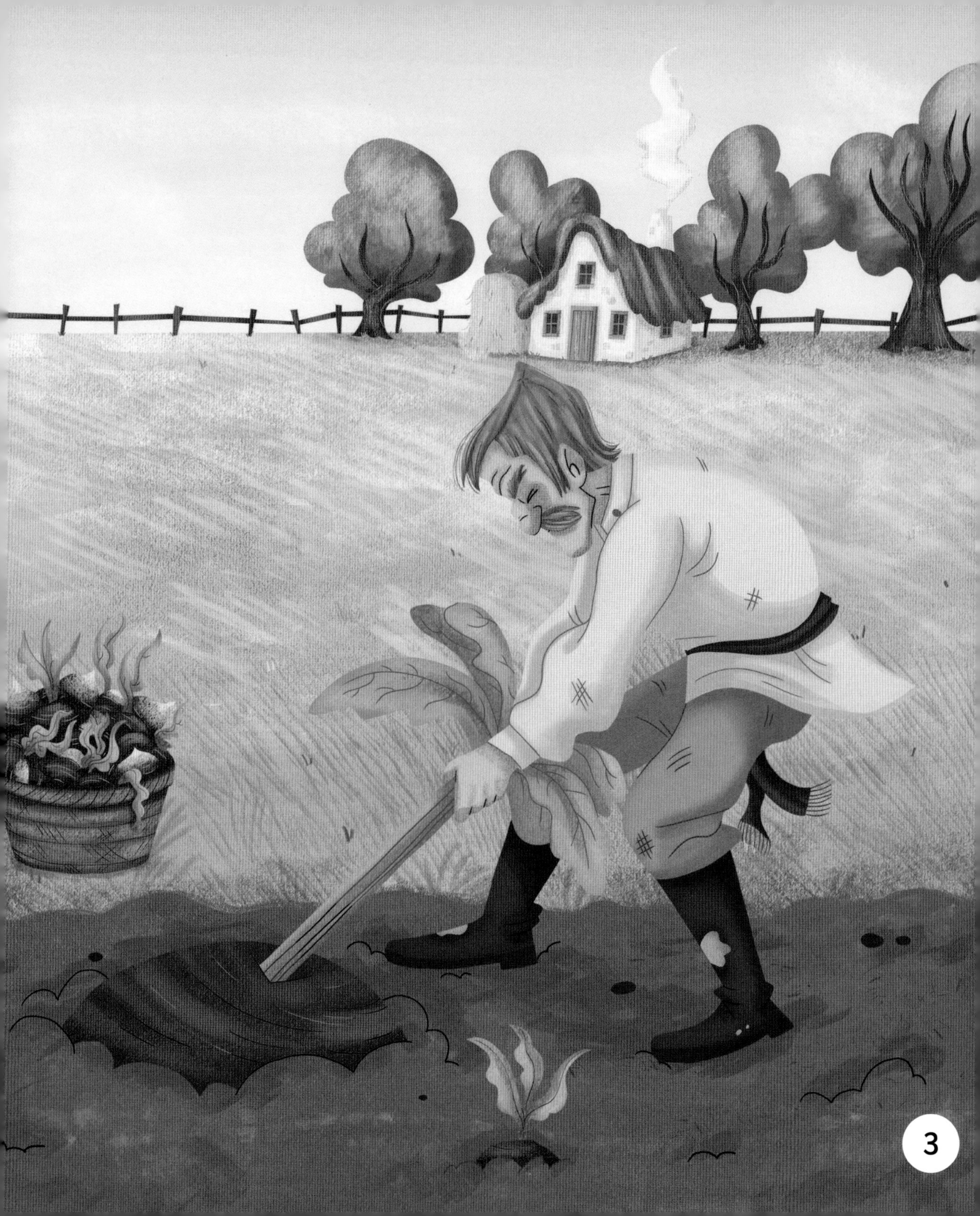

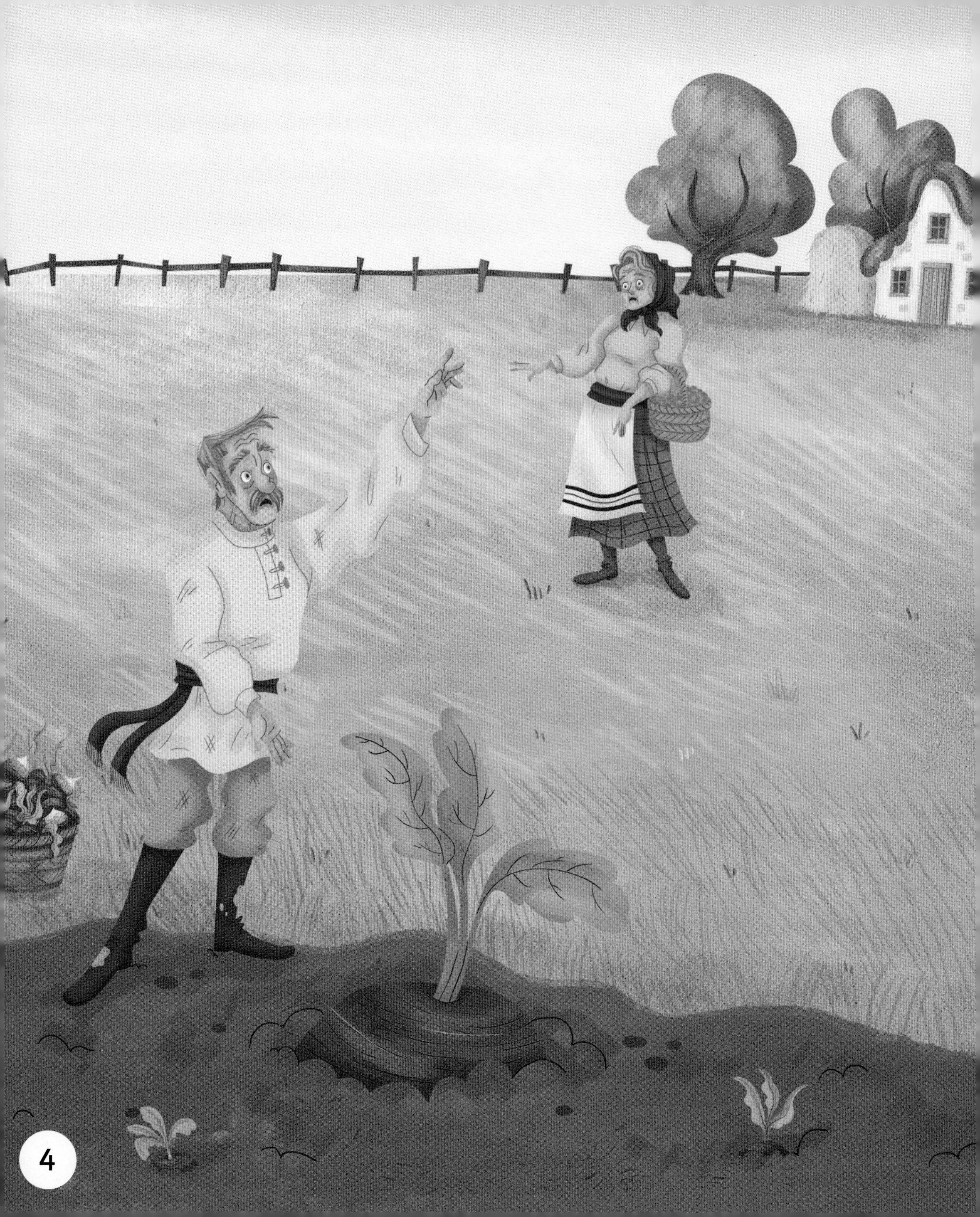

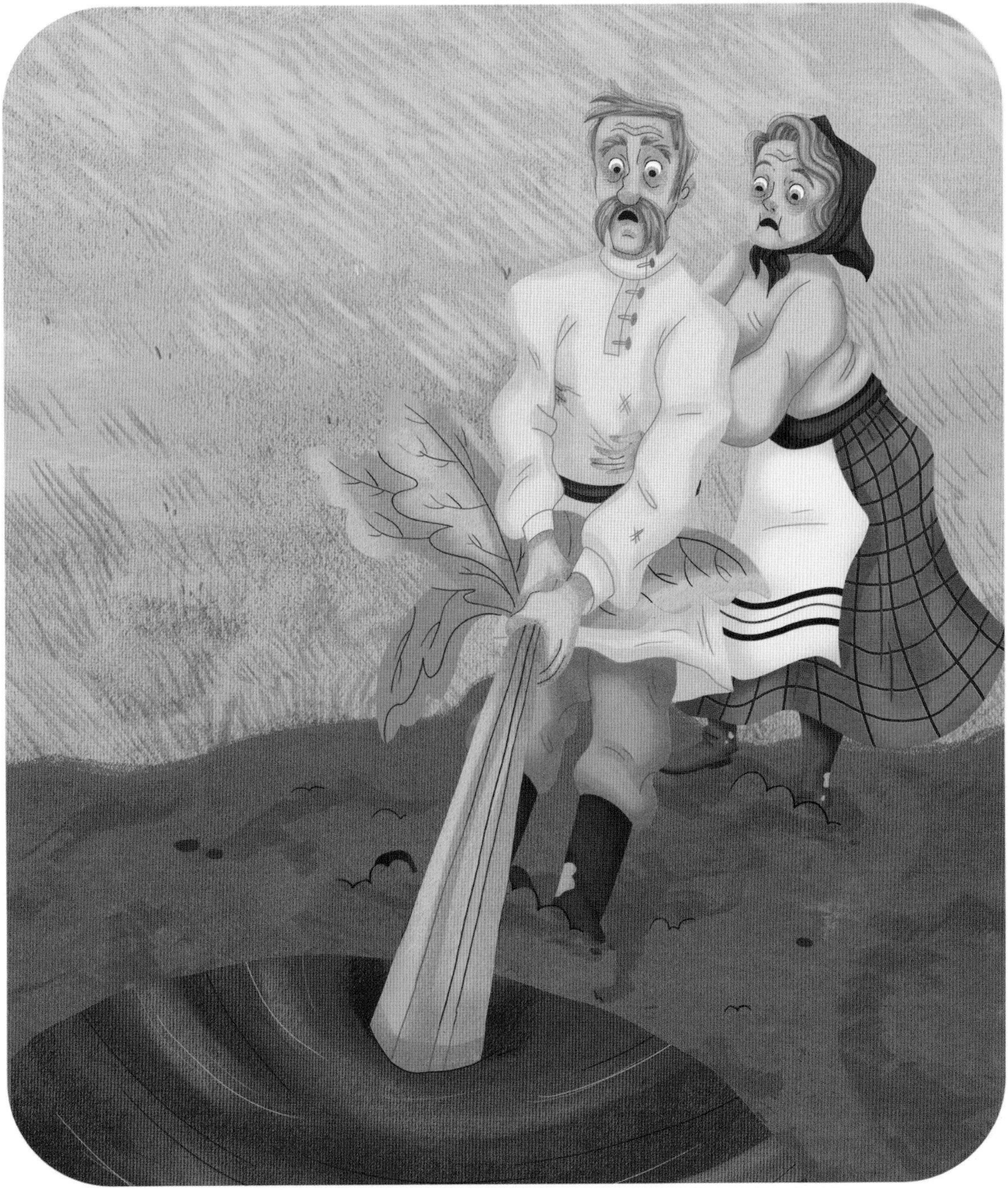

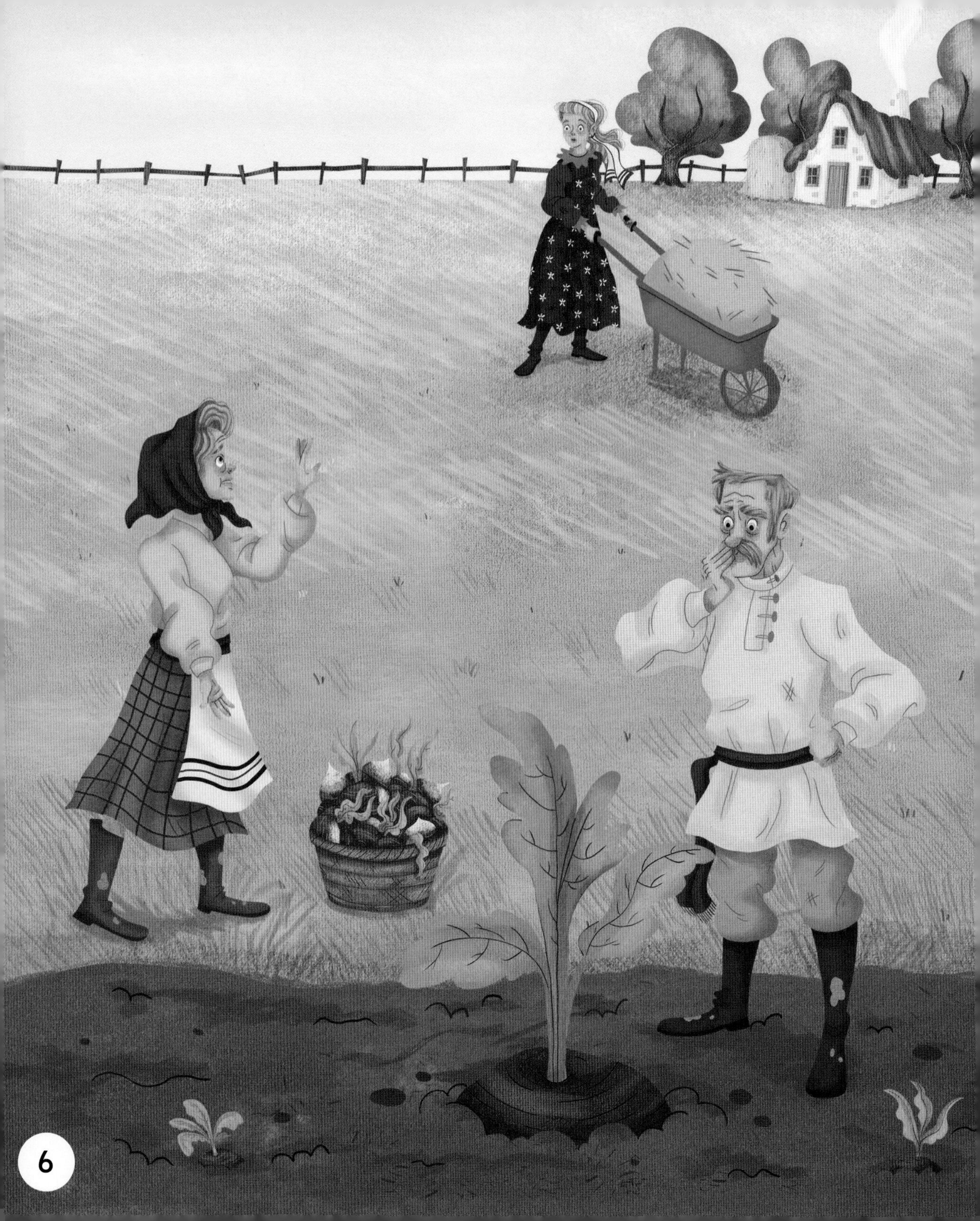

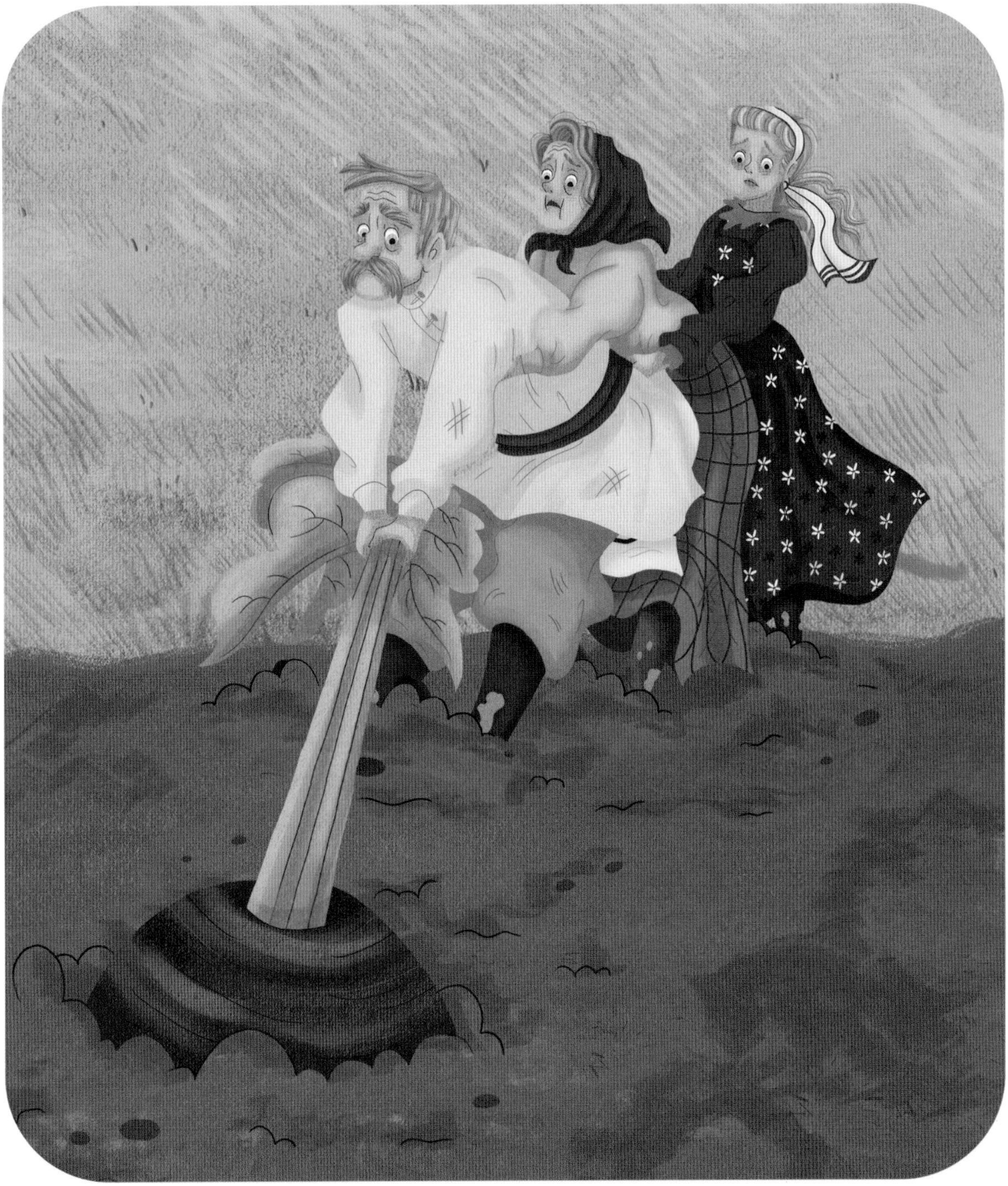

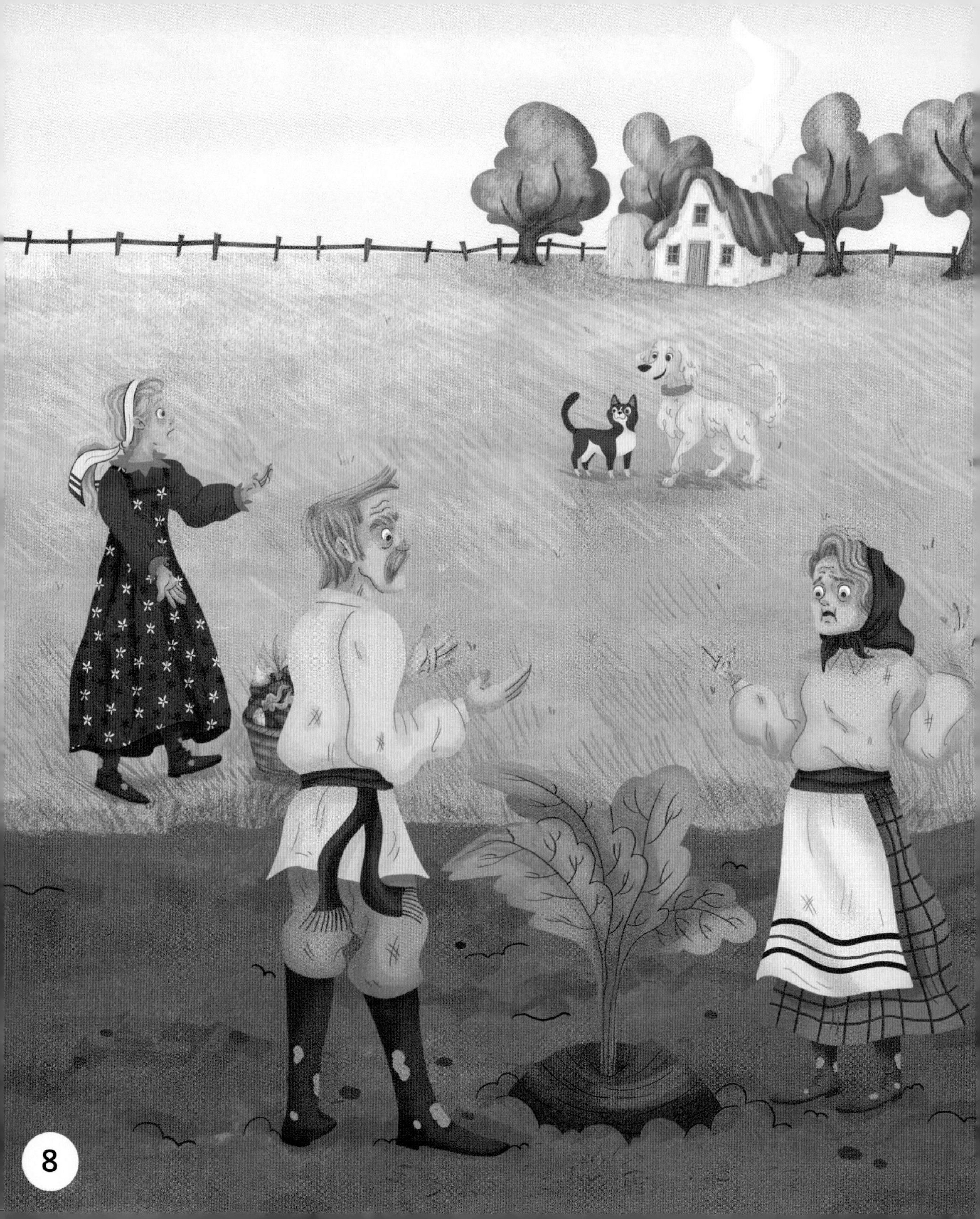

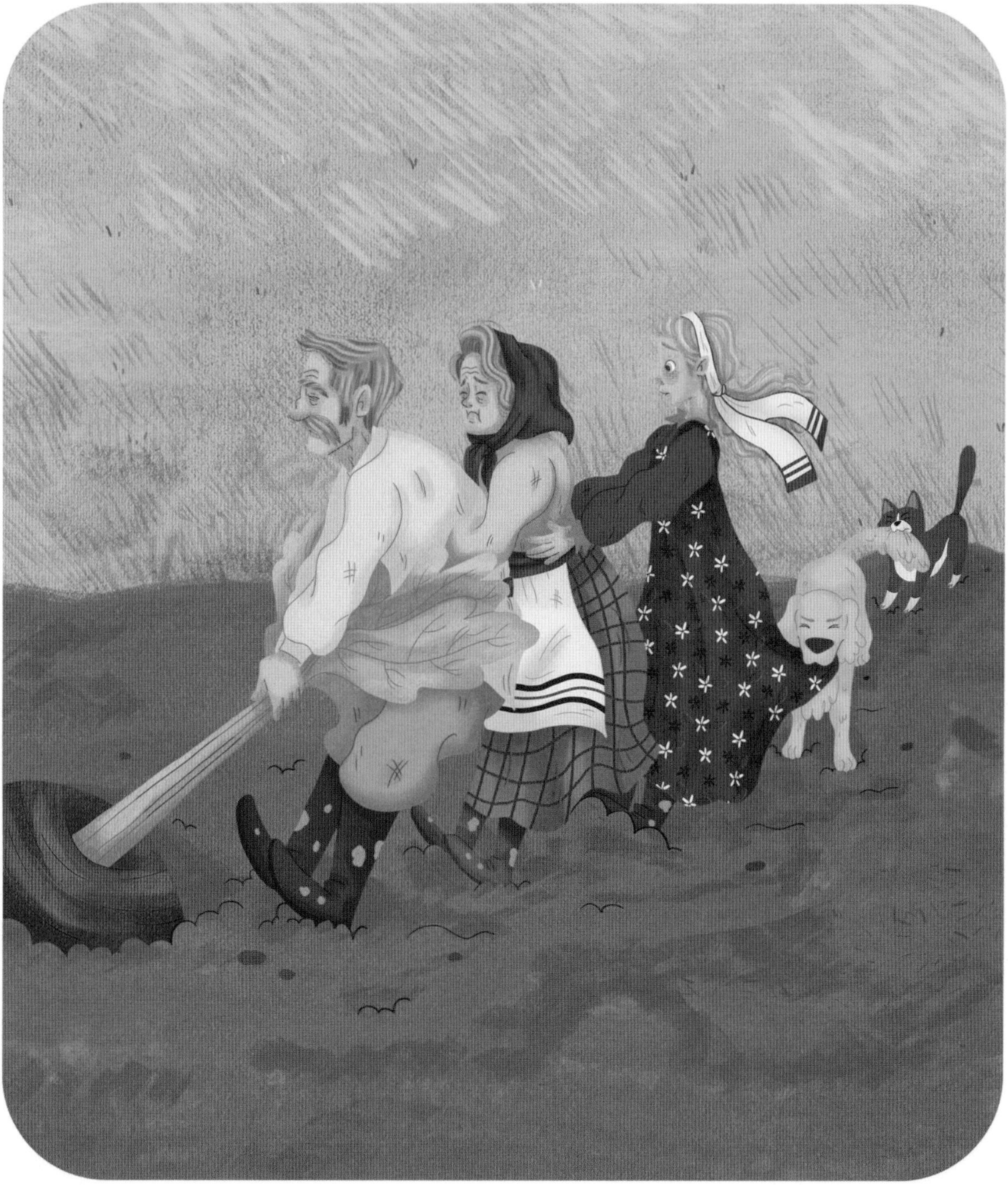

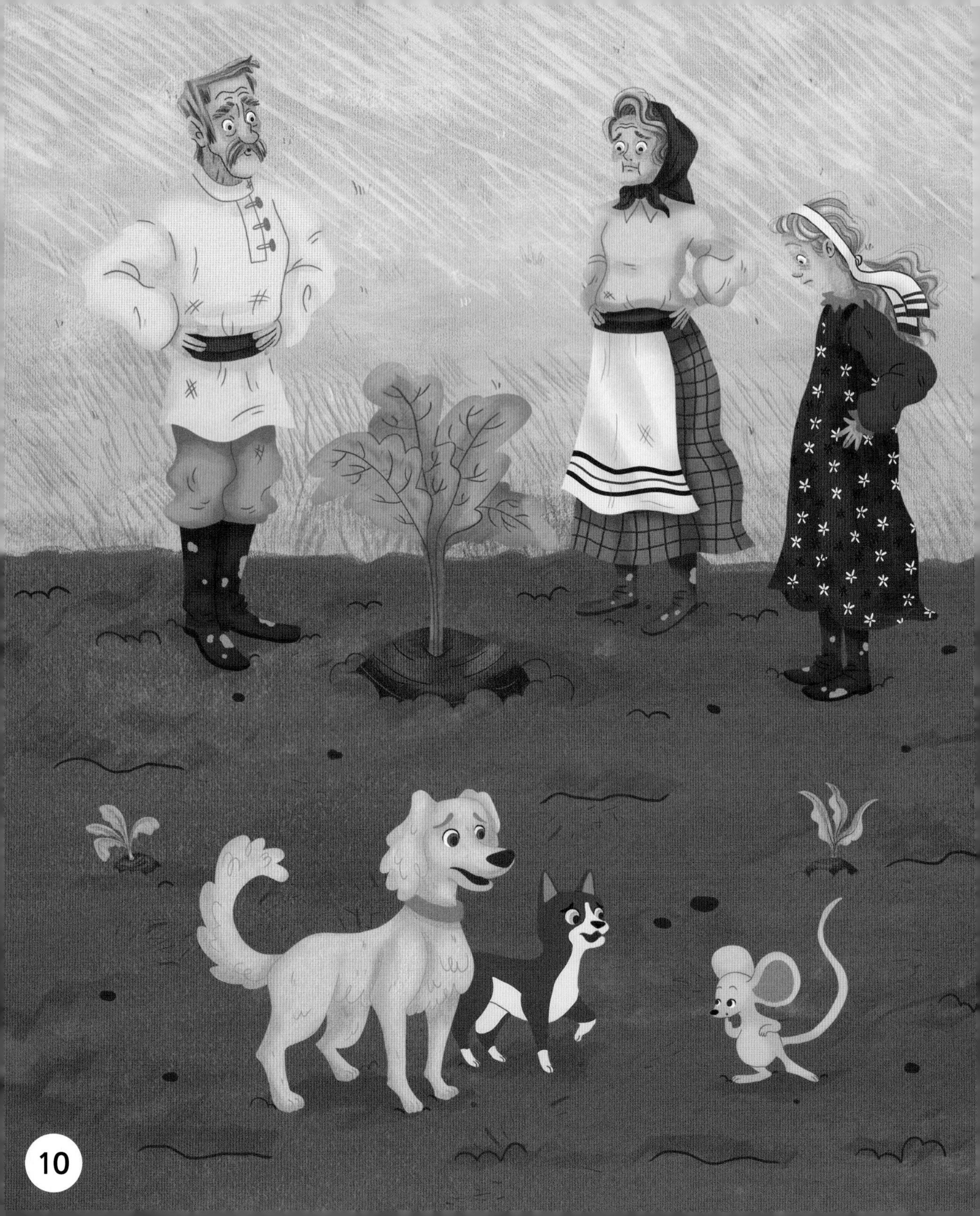

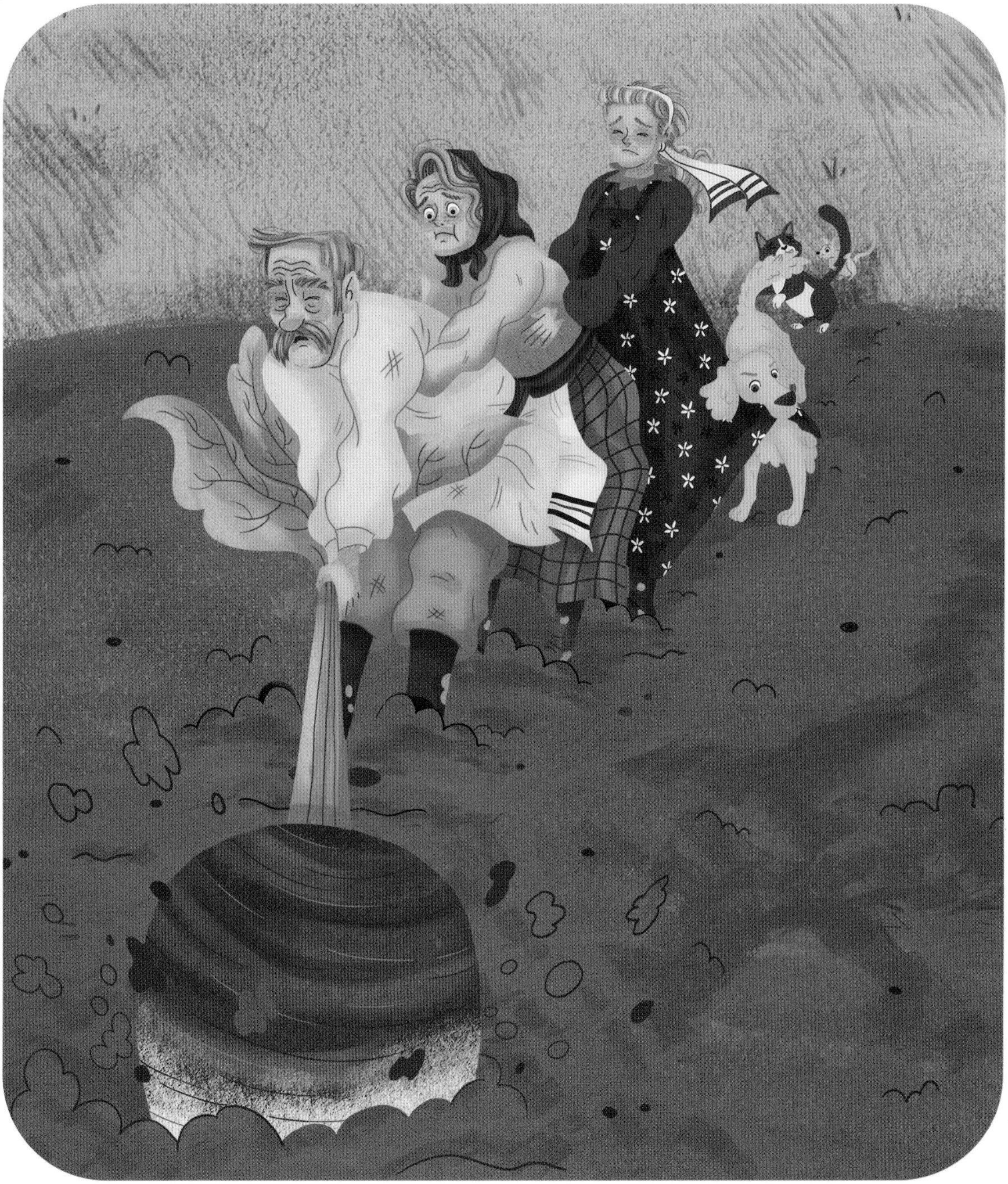

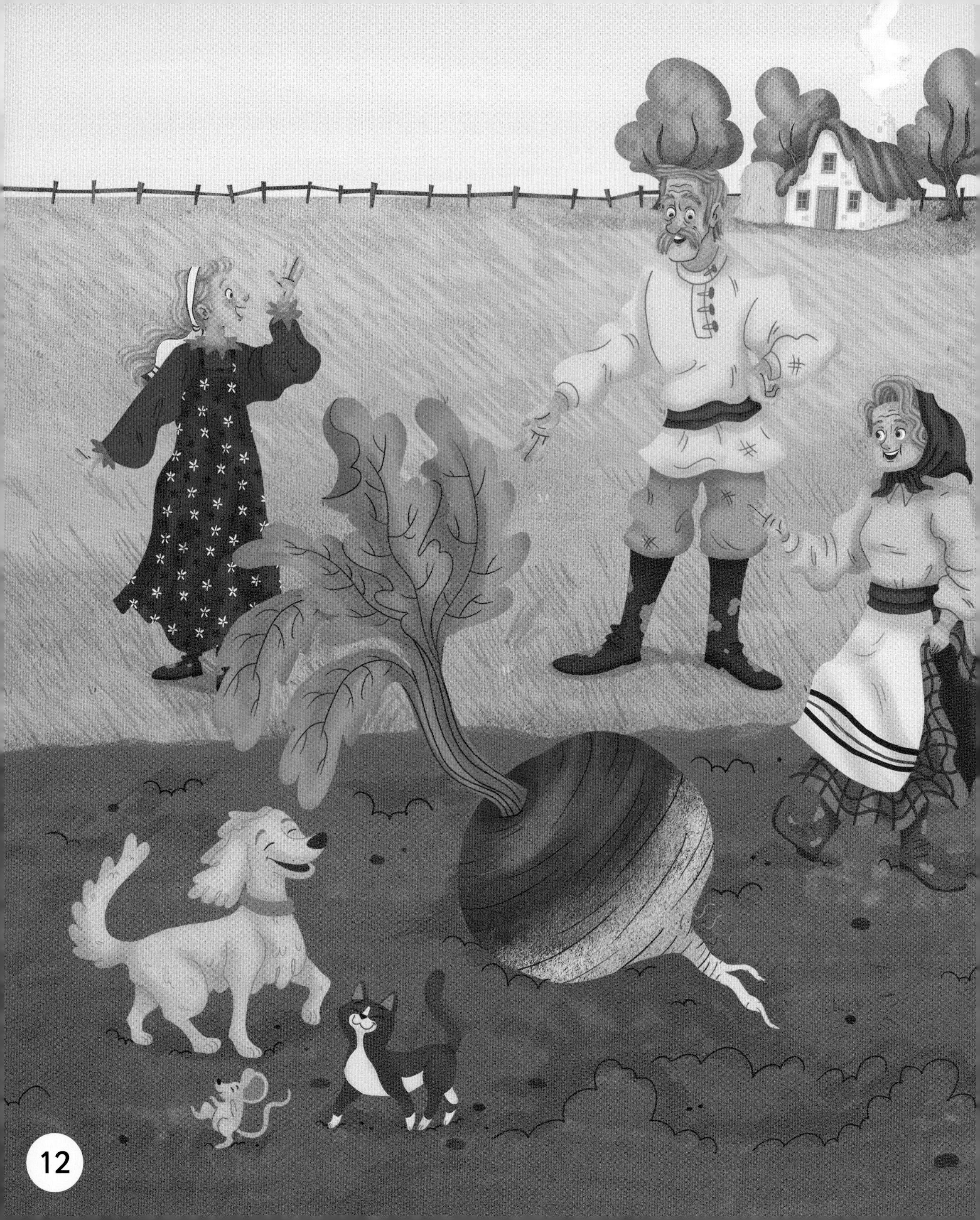